SOUNDBITES

Strings

Roger Thomas

Heinemann Library
Chicago, Illinois

© 2002 Reed Educational & Professional Publishing
Published by Heinemann Library,
an imprint of Reed Educational & Professional Publishing,
Chicago, Illinois

Customer Service 888-454-2279

Visit our website at www.heinemannlibrary.com

Designed by Paul Davies and Associates
Originated by Ambassador Litho Ltd.
Printed at Wing King Tong in Hong Kong

06 05 04 03 02
10 9 8 7 6 5 4 3 2 1

Library of Congress Cataloging-in-Publication Data
Thomas, Roger, 1956-
    Strings / Roger Thomas.
        p. cm. -- (Soundbites)
Includes bibliographical references (p.   ) and index.
    ISBN 1-58810-266-1
    1. Stringed instruments--Juvenile literature. [1. Stringed instruments.] I. Title. II. Series.
    ML750 .T46 2001
    787'.19--dc21
                                        2001001726

Acknowledgments
The author and publishers are grateful to the following for permission to reproduce copyright material:
Cover photograph: Redferns/Outline.
pp. 4, 8, 11, 13, 17, 22, 24, 25, 27 Redferns; pp. 5, 7, 12, 14 Photodisc; pp. 6, 9, 18, 21, 26 Lebrecht Picture Library; p. 10 Trevor Clifford; pp. 15, 16 Corbis; p. 19 Robert Harding Picture Library; p. 20 Musicmaker's Kits Inc.; p. 23 South American Pictures; p. 28 Outline Press; p. 29 The New Violin Family Assoc. Inc.

Special thanks to Jennifer Baker for her comments in the preparation of this book.

Every effort has been made to contact copyright holders of any material reproduced in this book. Any omissions will be rectified in subsequent printings if notice is given to the publisher.

Some words are shown in bold, **like this.** You can find out what they mean by looking in the glossary.

Contents

Introduction

Stringed instruments have a very long history in most cultures of the world. One instrument that originated in Africa, a **bow** with a **resonator** attached, is probably one of the oldest musical instruments of all.

A symphony orchestra's string section includes many violins, as well as violas, cellos, and double basses.

Bowed strings

Today, stringed instruments are used in all kinds of music throughout the world. Many of them, like the violin, viola, cello, and double **bass,** are played by moving a bow across the strings. In European and American classical music, these four instruments make up the string section of a **symphony orchestra.** They are played in other, smaller classical music groups as well. The violin is also used extensively in various kinds of folk music and has been adopted into Indian classical music (where it is sometimes played upright on the player's lap). Both the violin, double bass, and sometimes other strings are used in jazz. A string section is also often used in some rock and pop music to fill out the sound and provide background.

Plucked and stopped strings

The guitar is possibly the most widely recognized musical instrument in the world today. One popular type, the classical guitar, originally had strings made from animal gut, but now usually has nylon strings. Some steel-string guitars developed from the classical guitar, including the various types of **acoustic** guitars used in folk, jazz, and rock music. When the steel-string guitar was modified with **electronic pickups,** the result was the electric guitar, one of the most important instruments in rock and pop music.

The guitar is related to the **lute,** an earlier instrument that was developed from a medieval Persian instrument, the oud. The lute is also related to various other European and Middle Eastern instruments, such as the Greek **bouzouki.** The banjo, ukulele, and **mandolin** are very different instruments that originated in completely different parts of the world, yet they all work on the same basic principle as the lute and guitar. The notes made by these instruments are changed by **"stopping"**—holding down a string onto the **neck** with one hand to change the notes while the other hand plucks the string to sound the notes. Each of these instruments is used in music of its own particular culture, but they can also be used in lots of other different kinds of music. For example, the bouzouki is now popular in English folk music.

The electric guitar is a modern addition to the string family.

Harps and **lyres** are also played by plucking. Their strings are not stopped by the player's fingers, but are allowed to vibrate along their full length.

Other strings
Some stringed instruments are played using more unusual methods. You will find out more about these instruments as you read this book.

How Stringed Instruments Work

All stringed instruments, throughout history and the world, work in the same basic way. One or more strings is stretched between two firm anchor points on the instrument and then tightened. When it is plucked, rubbed, or struck, the string vibrates. We hear this vibration as sound.

Making the sound

Most strings do not vibrate loudly enough to be heard clearly on their own. For this reason, most stringed instruments also include some form of **resonator,** or **soundbox**—usually some sort of hollow chamber in the instrument. However, it is not really empty; it is full of air. While the string does not vibrate powerfully enough to be heard by itself, it is powerful enough to send sound waves vibrating through the air in the soundbox. The sound we hear is the sound of the vibrating air added to the sound of the string.

There are some exceptions to this. The simplest form of a musical **bow** does not have a resonator attached, but the player provides one by placing one end of the bow in his or her mouth. Some zithers have detachable soundboxes. Electric guitars, electric **bass** guitars, and other electronically **amplified** string instruments often have solid bodies instead of soundboxes. These do resonate to a certain extent, but the sound is amplified electronically so that it is loud enough to be heard in a musical performance.

The viol comes from the early fifteenth century. It is played with a bow but, unlike the violin family, the viol also uses **frets** to help produce accurate notes.

Changing the sound

Stringed instruments usually have some sort of mechanism built into them for tightening their strings. One of the easiest methods is to simply pull the string as tightly as possible, then slide one or more objects under the string to lift it away from the instrument's body and pull it even tighter at the same time. This method is used on an instrument called a ground zither, found in Africa and Southeast Asia. It has a string stretched across a bark-covered pit dug into the ground. Most other stringed instruments have a rotating peg at one end of each string. Some, like the violin and many folk harps, have wooden pegs that are fitted tightly into holes. Others, such as the guitar and double bass, have a system of metal **gears** to tighten the string smoothly. Some others, such as the **psaltery,** have a wrenchlike key to tighten the strings.

There are several different ways of producing a range of notes on a stringed instrument. There can be a string for each note, as with the Middle Eastern **qanun.** The strings may be stretched while playing, as with the concert harp and some types of electric guitars. The strings can be "shortened" by **stopping,** as with most guitars, or by pressing an object against them, as with the steel or Hawaiian guitar. **Harmonics** can also be used, as with the Egyptian folk harp.

The viola is slightly larger than the violin, with rounder, higher shoulders.

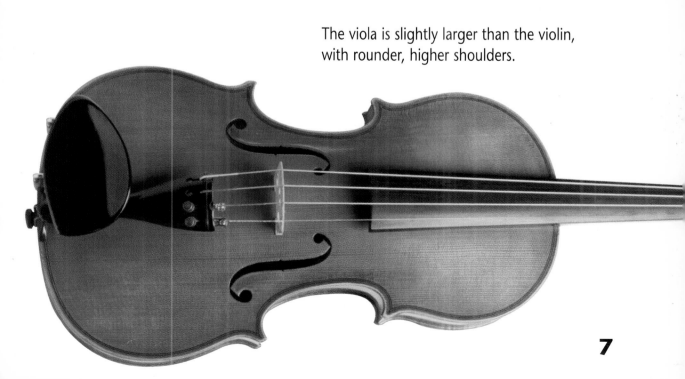

The Parts of a Stringed Instrumen

Stringed instruments generally fall into two groups: those with **necks** and those without. Instruments like the dulcimer and harp have no necks. They consist of strings stretched across a frame or box. Instruments with necks include the guitar, **bass** guitar, banjo, violin, viola, cello, double bass, and many others. Each has a similar set of parts that have the same function, although they may be used to make very different kinds of music. The easiest way to identify the parts is to follow the strings from one end of the instrument to the other.

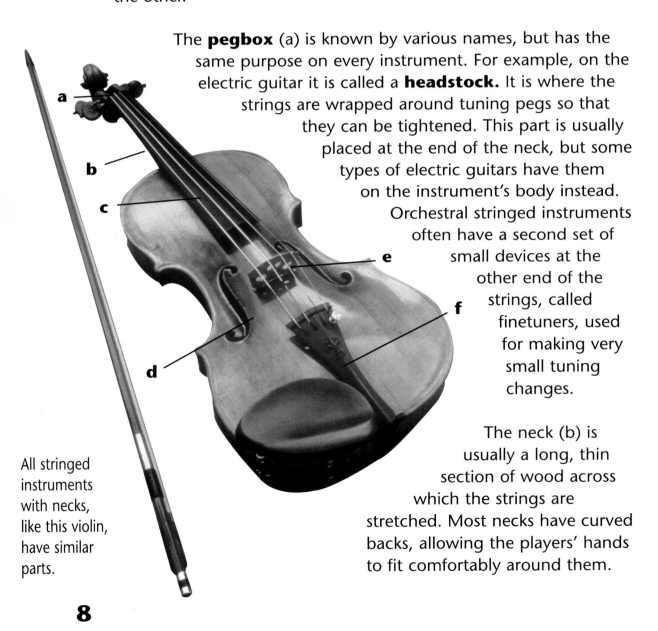

The **pegbox** (a) is known by various names, but has the same purpose on every instrument. For example, on the electric guitar it is called a **headstock.** It is where the strings are wrapped around tuning pegs so that they can be tightened. This part is usually placed at the end of the neck, but some types of electric guitars have them on the instrument's body instead. Orchestral stringed instruments often have a second set of small devices at the other end of the strings, called finetuners, used for making very small tuning changes.

The neck (b) is usually a long, thin section of wood across which the strings are stretched. Most necks have curved backs, allowing the players' hands to fit comfortably around them.

All stringed instruments with necks, like this violin, have similar parts.

8

The **fingerboard** (c) is a smooth piece of wood, usually on the front of the neck. The player presses the strings down onto this to change the notes. Some fingerboards on stringed instruments may have **frets.** On most guitars, they are small strips of wire attached to the fingerboard. Other instruments, such as the violin family, have no frets (although the related viol family does use them). Frets have two effects on the instrument. First, they produce very accurate notes, because the string is always pulled onto the fret in the same position. Second, they keep the player's fingertips from muffling the sound of the string, making the **tone** of the instrument clearer and brighter.

Stringed instruments without necks have some parts that look and work like those on instruments with necks, but they are often played differently.

The **soundbox** (d) is a hollow box that **amplifies** the sound. Most nonelectric stringed instruments use a soundbox to help their sound be heard.

The **bridge** (e) is a hard edge that the strings are pulled over, giving a precise point beyond which the strings cannot vibrate. The ends of the strings may then be attached to a **tailpiece** (f) on the end of the instrument or may be anchored behind the bridge.

The Violin and the Viola

The violin and the viola are the two highest-**pitched** stringed instruments in the classical orchestra. The violin is also used in many other forms of music, including jazz and folk music. Many different musical cultures across the world use instruments similar to the violin. The violin and viola are played with a **bow** that has horsehair (or a man-made substitute) attached along its length. A sticky substance called **rosin** is rubbed onto the horsehair, causing the strings to vibrate when the bow is drawn across them. The instruments are held under the player's chin.

Classical music

These two instruments are used in several different ways in classical music. For example, there are two sections of violins in a **symphony orchestra,** known as the first and second violins. Each section has a different part to play. There is only one section of violas in a symphony orchestra, all playing the same part. There is also a form of music called the **concerto,** in which an instrumental **soloist** is featured with an orchestra. There are many concertos written for the violin, and some for the viola, too.

The viola has a lower pitch than the violin, but is played in a similar way.

Violins and violas may also be featured, either alone or with other instruments, in small groups of instrumentalists called **chamber ensembles.** There are also smaller groups for string players, such as the **string quartet.** This kind of group usually includes two violins, one viola, and one cello.

Yehudi Menuhin was a **virtuoso** violin player.

Sometimes, a single instrument may be featured, generally with piano accompaniment, in a piece of music called a **sonata.** Many composers have written sonatas for the violin, and some have been written for the viola as well.

Jazz, rock, folk, and world music

The violin can also be used in traditional, "fusion" (a cross between jazz and rock music), and **avant-garde** jazz. The viola, with its deeper, "darker" sound, is not popular in these areas of music. However, this quality has meant that some rock bands, such as the Velvet Underground, have found the viola to be an interesting addition to their sound. The violin is sometimes used in rock music, either as a solo instrument (mostly in electric "folk-rock") or as part of a string section backing a rock band (this may also include violas). The violin is used extensively in "pure" folk music forms, ranging from **Cajun** to **Gaelic** music. The violin has also become an important instrument in Indian music.

Electric instruments

The use of the violin in nonclassical music has led to the development of electric violins with solid bodies like those of most electric guitars. One type, designed by Indian violinist L. Shankar, has two **necks** with different tunings.

The Cello and the Double Bass

The cello and the double **bass** play the second-lowest and lowest ranges of notes in the string section of a **symphony** or **chamber orchestra.** Like the violin and viola, they are also used in other forms of classical music, playing **concertos** and **sonatas,** and being part of chamber **ensembles.**

Unlike the violin and viola, however, these instruments are played vertically. A cellist normally sits on a chair, holding the body of the instrument between his or her knees, with the weight of the instrument resting on an endpin. The double bass is a larger instrument, and a classical player will often sit on a high stool to play it. The body of the double bass rests on the floor on an endpin attached to the bottom of the instrument. Occasionally, the player may choose to stand while playing the instrument. This playing position is popular with jazz bassists.

The endpin supporting a cello can be adjusted to the height needed by the cellist.

Bowing and plucking

In classical music, both the cello and the double bass are usually played with a **bow,** although sometimes there will be parts of the music where the strings have to be plucked with the fingers. This technique, called **pizzicato,** is also used by classical violin and viola players. Jazz bassists are more often required to play their instrument by plucking and slapping the strings than by using a bow. For this reason, many jazz players keep the bow in a holster attached to the tailpiece of the bass until they need it.

Variations

The cello has not changed very much since it first began to replace an earlier instrument, the *bass viola de bracchio,* in the early 1600s. However, these early cellos had five strings, while the modern cello has only four.

The double bass has been experimented with in many different ways. Although the cello and the double bass look similar, the double bass was developed from the viol family rather than from the *bass viola de bracchio.* Many double basses have lower "shoulders" that are more like a bass viol's than like anything from the violin family. Some double basses have five strings instead of four. There are also devices called extensions that can be attached to the **pegbox** to allow one of the strings to be slightly longer, so that lower notes can be played.

Double basses are popular with jazz artists.

Electric instruments

Some manufacturers have made electric cellos, including one folding model designed for easy transport. However, various types of electric double basses have existed since the 1950s. Some have bodies that are completely or partly hollow, making them look fairly similar to the standard double bass (although they are often finished in very bright colors). Other solid-bodied instruments can have more unusual shapes. These instruments are usually used by jazz and rock musicians, many of whom started out by playing the bass guitar.

Fretted Instruments

There are many kinds of **fretted** instruments in use around the world. The guitar is one of the most important and is made in many designs.

Types of guitars

The classical guitar is used to play **solo, ensemble,** and **concerto** music from the classical **repertoire.** It usually has six nylon strings (some models have more than this) that are plucked with the fingernails. Earlier versions, such as the smaller **Baroque** guitar, are still used for playing period music.

The folk guitar is also known simply as the **acoustic** guitar, to distinguish it from the electric guitar. It is similar to the Spanish guitar, but is often larger and has steel strings. It is often played with a **pick.** Variations include a twelve-stringed version; a version with a curved, plastic body; and a version with a metal plate on the front of the body that gives the instrument a sharp, cutting **tone.**

The archtop, or cello guitar, looks a little like a cello with a **neck** tilted away from the body and "f"-shaped sound holes. It was designed to replace the banjo in dance bands, and it is also popular as a jazz instrument.

The electric guitar is used mainly in rock, pop, and jazz music, and is one of the most popular guitars in the world. The sound of the strings is transmitted by **electronic pickups** to an **amplifier.** Most have solid bodies, but some electric archtop guitars have full-sized or slightly shallower hollow bodies. These are most popular as jazz instruments.

The **bass** guitar plays lower notes than the electric guitar and has thicker, heavier strings. Originally invented as an alternative to the double bass, the bass guitar also traditionally has four strings. There are versions with five, six, or even more strings, as well as smaller "short-scale" designs that some players prefer. Some bass guitars are electric and others acoustic. There are also fretless models that have a tone similar to that of the double bass.

The Chinese mandolin is one of a huge variety of fretted instruments in use around the world today.

Other fretted instruments

The larger family of fretted instruments includes the banjo, with its drumlike body; the **mandolin,** a small kind of steel-strung **lute;** the mandola, a large type of mandolin; the Indian sitar, with large, movable frets; and the ukulele, a Hawaiian instrument that looks like a small, four-stringed Spanish guitar. There are also combination instruments, such as the banjolin and banjolele. These have banjolike bodies, but have necks and strings like the mandolin and the ukulele, respectively.

Innovative instruments

New fretted instruments are still being invented. These have included the sitar-guitar (a guitar with a sitarlike tone), and the Chapman Stick, an electric instrument that is played by "hammering'"the strings against the frets with the fingers.

Harps and Lyres

Harps and **lyres** are part of a very ancient group of instruments. Pictures of them have been found on fragments of pottery dating back to 3300 B.C.E. There have been many variations and refinements in the design of these instruments over the centuries, but they still work in the same basic way.

Harp or lyre?

The main difference between a harp and a lyre is in the way each is made. A harp is basically triangular in shape, while a lyre is a rectangle. On a harp, the strings run from one side of the triangle to another, but a lyre's strings run from one end of the rectangle to the opposite end. On both harps and lyres, one end of each string is usually attached to a **soundbox** that forms a part of the instrument.

Lyres

Various forms of lyres were played in Europe during the Middle Ages, often to accompany singing. Most were plucked, but a few, like the Welsh crwth, were played with a **bow.** Today, the lyre survives in only a few cultures, such as in Africa, where many different designs of lyres are played in Egypt, the Sudan, Kenya, Uganda, and elsewhere.

Lyres were more commonly used in ancient times. Few are seen in today's modern cultures.

Types of harps

The concert or pedal harp is the type of harp usually used for performances of classical music. It is played in **symphony orchestras,** in some **chamber ensembles,** as a **solo** instrument, and as an accompanying instrument. The strings that the player plucks with his or her fingers are tuned at the instrument's top. The soundbox is at the bottom of the instrument. There is a set of pedals at the base of the instrument that can change the **tension** of the strings, making a wider range of notes available.

The clarsach is a traditional Celtic harp that originated in Ireland. It is similar in shape to the concert harp, but is smaller, with fewer strings and no pedals. It is sometimes used as an instrument for people who want to learn how to play the concert harp. Its name means "little flat thing," despite the fact that it is vertical and quite large!

Double and triple harps were developed during the sixteenth and seventeenth centuries, before the invention of the pedal harp, in an attempt to allow the harp to have more playable notes. The double harp had two rows of strings, each with a different tuning. The triple harp had two outer sets of strings with the same tuning and a middle set of strings tuned to the "missing" notes. This made it easier to reach the correct notes with either hand.

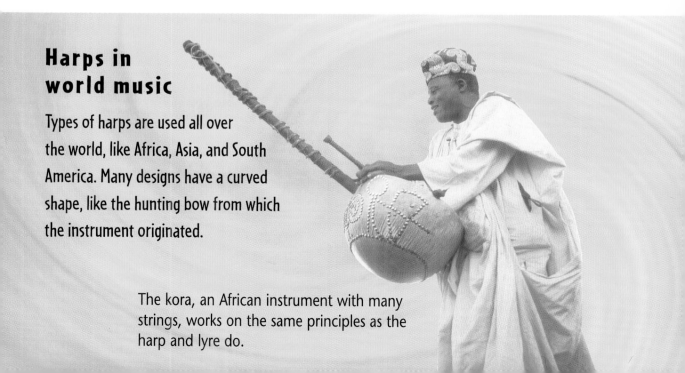

Harps in world music

Types of harps are used all over the world, like Africa, Asia, and South America. Many designs have a curved shape, like the hunting bow from which the instrument originated.

The kora, an African instrument with many strings, works on the same principles as the harp and lyre do.

Zithers

Zithers are types of stringed instruments on which the strings run from one end to the other, often (but not always) with no **frets** or other means of changing the note of a single string. These instruments are played by plucking. They are similar to dulcimers, except that dulcimers are usually played with hammers.

Simple zithers

The simplest zithers illustrate the most important principles of stringed instruments very well. In Africa, there are trough zithers, which are each made of a hollowed-out piece of wood with strings stretched across the hollow area. The result looks like an animal feeding trough, thus the name. Sometimes one long continuous string is used, stretched backwards and forwards across the trough. Tube zithers are traditional in some parts of Africa and Eastern Europe. They can be made of wood or cane and usually consist of a single hollow cylinder with a slot cut in it to let the sound out.

Some zithers are very sophisticated. The vina, an Indian instrument, comes in several different designs. The most basic design consists of a hollow tube with strings stretched along it and a **gourd soundbox** at one end. There are also other types that have many strings and frets.

The Japanese koto is one type of zither with a very distinctive sound.

One or two strings are then tied to the ends of the instrument, with a small **bridge** placed under each end of the strings to help give a clear sound. On some tube zithers, the "string" is formed from the material that has been cut for the slot. It is left attached at each end of the slot, and small bridges are forced underneath it to raise and tighten the "string."

More complex zithers

The Japanese koto has movable bridges that can be slid up and down the instrument to change the notes. By pressing a string down on one side of the bridge while plucking it on the other side, the player can raise the **pitch** of the note slightly. This gives a distorted "bending" effect similar to that produced on an electric guitar. Other instruments similar to the koto include the kayakeum from Korea and the ch'in from China.

The European zither

The European zither is usually box-shaped, with a set of tuning pegs at one end. It is a popular folk instrument in many countries, especially in Eastern Europe, and has a long history. One very early example is the **psaltery,** developed from a Middle Eastern zither that was first brought to Europe in the eleventh century. One European zither played in the fourteenth and fifteenth centuries had a triangular shape with sound holes in each corner. It was said to remind people of a pig's head and was known as *strumento di porco,* meaning "pig instrument."

Dulcimers

Dulcimers are similar to zithers, except that instead of being plucked, the strings are usually struck with hammers or beaters. This means that the dulcimer is a percussion instrument as well. It also has similarities to two keyboard instruments that work by having strings struck with hammers—the piano and the **clavichord.**

Instruments from many lands

Like the zither, the dulcimer came to Europe from the Middle East in the eleventh century. It was very popular from the seventeenth to the nineteenth centuries, but it is now mostly used for playing traditional music. Different kinds of dulcimers found in the musical traditions of many countries include the Iraqi santir, the Russian chang, the Indian santoor, and the Korean yangum.

The Chinese yang-ch'in is more unusual. The yang-ch'in was introduced to China from the **West** in about 1800. It became an important feature in Chinese orchestras and accompaniments. The Chinese name for this instrument actually means "foreign."

Dulcimer or zither?

The most widely heard instrument known as a dulcimer today is not really a dulcimer at all, but a type of **fretted** zither. The Appalachian dulcimer is an elegant instrument with a narrow **fingerboard.** The strings are plucked rather than struck. It is used in several forms of folk music, particularly in the United States.

The Appalachian dulcimer, shown here, is really a zither.

A classical dulcimer

The cimbalom is a fairly large dulcimer from Hungary. The design of the cimbalom was improved in the 1860s so that it could play a wider range of notes. **Dampers** were also added to allow the player to change the instrument's **tone.** This change made it suitable for use in classical music. The Hungarian composer Zoltán Kodály used it in his well-known opera *Háry János* in 1927. In classical music, the cimbalom is usually played by a percussionist, because the use of hammers and beaters is a percussion technique.

The cimbalom is mainly used by central European Gypsies in their folk music.

Dulcimer beaters

Various different kinds of beaters are used for playing instruments from the dulcimer family, depending on the traditions of the music being played. The three main styles of beaters are straight sticks, sticks with curved ends, and sticks with padded ends that give a softer sound. Because the strings give the instrument a "bouncy" response, a skilled player can produce very fast and complicated tunes on the instrument.

An extra-large dulcimer

At the end of the seventeenth century, a German musician named Pantaleon Hebenstreit built a very large dulcimer that became known as the pantaleon. The instrument was eleven feet (3.4 meters) long, with two soundboards and quadruple sets of strings. Hebenstreit composed several successful works for the instrument.

Other Kinds of Stringed Instruments

Many of the stringed instruments used in the **West** are based on instruments from other parts of the world, such as the guitar and the **lute.** However, there are many other non-Western stringed instruments that remain unique to the musical cultures in which they originated.

The sitar is probably the best-known instrument from India. It is large, similar to a lute, with a bowl-shaped wooden **soundbox** at the bottom and usually another made from a dried **gourd** at the top. The sitar has two sets of strings. One set consists of seven strings that are plucked with a **pick.** The notes on five of these strings can be changed by pressing them against movable metal **frets** on the sitar's large **neck.** As with the Japanese koto, the player can add a "bending" sound to the notes. The other two strings are **drone strings.** They are not **stopped** on the frets, so they will always give the same notes. Beneath these seven strings are twelve or more **sympathetic strings** that the player does not touch. Instead, the strings are made to vibrate by the sound of the top set of strings. This gives the instrument its unique sound.

The saranghi is a small **bowed** Indian instrument that is held in front of the player. Like the sitar, it has a set of sympathetic strings. It is unusual in that the strings are stopped using the cuticles of the player's fingernails.

The Indian sitar has a unique sound. This is Ravi Shankar, a famous Indian sitarist.

The charango

When Spanish travelers first reached South America, they brought with them examples of a guitarlike instrument called the *vihuela*. The native inhabitants copied the idea, but instead of using wood to make the soundbox, they used the shell of a small animal called an armadillo. This version of the instrument, still used today by South American folk groups, became known as the charango. Some other versions have more conventional wooden soundboxes.

An armadillo's shell gives the charango a distinctive look and sound.

Long thought of as the national instrument of Russia, the balalaika first became known in Europe in the seventeenth century. It is a type of lute, with three strings and an unusual triangular soundbox. There are six different sizes, all of which are used in large balalaika bands.

The pi-pa, one of many Chinese plucked instruments, is a type of lute with a short neck and a distinctive teardrop shape. It has been known in China for about 2,000 years. It has four silk strings that produce a warm, clear **tone.**

The ramkie is an interesting example of how modern technology can be adapted to folk instruments. It is a type of simple, homemade folk guitar played in Southern Africa. Originally, these had soundboxes made from gourds or dried skin, but now tin cans are often used instead.

Strings in Jazz, Rock, and Pop

The guitar and **bass** guitar are the most widely used stringed instruments in rock and pop. In jazz, the double bass is also common. However, there are many other examples of string instruments being used in these forms of music.

Together with the double bass, the violin, viola, and cello are sometimes used to put together a complete orchestral string section to provide backing for rock and pop tunes. Sometimes just a **string quartet** will be used. This is an idea that goes in and out of fashion—it was popular during the 1950s and again during the 1990s. The violin, usually **amplified** or in the form of an electric instrument, is popular in electric "folk-rock" and is also used in jazz. The double bass is sometimes used in rock music in a deliberate "retro" style and some rock bassists use a solid-bodied, electric double bass. The whole range of orchestral string instruments can be used in **avant-garde** jazz.

The rock band Nirvana used a string section in some of their performances.

In the 1960s and 1970s, several rock bands including The Beatles and The Rolling Stones, were influenced by Indian music and used

Banjo music

The banjo is like a guitar, except that its **soundbox** has a front made of stretched **vellum** or plastic, like a drum. It probably evolved from African **lyres** that worked in a similar way. Its bright, loud sound made it popular in early dance and jazz bands. Today, the banjo is widely used in folk music in the United States and elsewhere, as well as in traditional jazz bands that aim to recreate the sounds of early jazz.

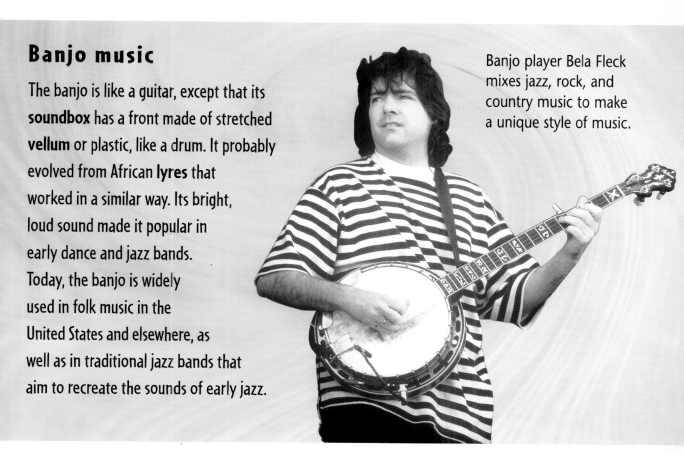

Banjo player Bela Fleck mixes jazz, rock, and country music to make a unique style of music.

sitars on some of their recordings. One guitar manufacturer also made several models of sitar-guitars. These were electric guitars with **sympathetic strings** and a special **bridge** that enabled them to make a sound like a sitar's. These instruments were easier for rock guitarists to play than true sitars.

The autoharp is a type of zither with sets of buttons that operate **dampers, muting** certain strings. By removing notes from the instrument's sound in this way, the player has a set of ready-made chords that can be strummed or plucked. This instrument has often been used by folk-rock musicians. More recently, musician Daniel Lanois has used a form of "high-tech" autoharp, with electronic sensors instead of strings.

Although normally associated with classical and folk music, the **mandolin** is occasionally used in rock and jazz as well. Some electric mandolins have been developed that work in the same way as the electric guitar.

String Recording and Performance Technology

Although the electric guitar and **bass** have become very important in today's music, nearly all stringed instruments began their history as **acoustic** instruments. There are very few exceptions to this rule—the Chapman Stick is one. However, the need to project the sound of the instruments to large audiences, together with the invention of sound recording, has given electronic technology an important place in the history of this family of instruments.

An early solution

Before the invention of electronic recording, music was recorded by placing a very large funnel-shaped horn in front of the musicians. The horn tapered down to a point that had a sharp needle on it. The needle vibrated when music was played into the horn, cutting a groove into a "master" disk (a wax cylinder was used for the earliest recordings). However, the delicate sound of stringed instruments did not record well this way. So in 1904, German inventor Augustus Stroh created a violin with a metal trumpetlike horn instead of a **soundbox.** This instrument could

Microphones have made it possible to record the sound of stringed instruments much more clearly.

project the sound straight into the recording horn. However, the **tone** of the instrument was not very good.

Strings and microphones

The development of microphones and electronic recording made it possible to record stringed instruments much more accurately. Various techniques have been used for recording orchestral string sections, ranging from placing a microphone above each instrument to simply placing one or two microphones in front of all the performers. Acoustic guitars and other **solo** string instruments are usually recorded with one or two microphones placed near the instrument, but for live performances, a type of microphone that attaches directly to the instrument is often used. This is called a transducer and is much less likely to pick up sound from outside the instrument. Some musicians use both techniques at once and mix the results, giving a full, pleasing sound.

The electric guitar

The electric guitar relies on **amplification** in performance. However, in the early days of the instrument, the amplifiers available would often produce feedback (a howling noise produced when the sound from the amplifier is picked up by the guitar) and a distorted sound. Guitarists began to use these "faults" on purpose as interesting aspects of their instruments' sound. Many modern amplifiers do not produce feedback, but there are electronic devices, often built into boxes with foot switches, that can produce this and many other changes to the guitar's sound electronically.

Electronic technology can be as important to the electric guitarist as the instrument itself.

Innovative Strings

Compared with other kinds of instruments—like the mechanism of the piano or the valve system of a brass instrument—stringed instruments are constructed quite simply. This makes them easy to modify and may be one reason why there have been so many ideas for creating more ways for stringed instruments to make sounds.

More necks, more strings

Some early **fretted** instruments, such as the theorbo (a form of **bass lute**), had extra strings that ran from the **soundbox** to the **pegbox** without passing directly over the **neck** and frets. Today, there are many models of electric guitars (and just a few **acoustic** designs) that have two necks, and a few have three or even more. Each type has different strings. The most popular combinations are a six-stringed and a twelve-stringed guitar neck or a six-stringed guitar neck and a four-stringed bass neck. All these combinations give players a bigger range of sounds.

This unique three-necked bass guitar has one fretless and two fretted necks, providing an interesting range of sounds.

A less elaborate development has been the addition of extra strings to single-necked guitars and bass guitars. There are seven-stringed guitars, twelve-stringed guitars with the strings arranged in six pairs, bass guitars with six or more strings, and many other variations.

New classical strings

In the 1950s, composer Henry Brant from the United States asked a violin maker, Dr. Carleen Hutchins, if she could redesign the stringed instruments used in classical music. Each of the four main instruments had evolved slightly differently, and their sizes and shapes were no longer in proper proportion. This meant that the instruments all had different **tones.** So a viola, for example, sounded quite different from a violin, instead of simply having a similar sound at a lower **pitch.** Dr. Hutchins designed a family of eight new instruments. The smallest was a **treble** violin, pitched an **octave** above a normal violin, and the largest was a **contrabass** violin, with the same lowest note as a double bass, but with a much larger body to give a fuller, richer tone. The instruments were praised by many musicians, including conductor Leopold Stokowski (who was featured in the animated Walt Disney film *Fantasia*). While they are not widely used, these designs of instruments are still being refined, and interested musicians continue to use them.

Dr. Carleen Hutchins's new string instrument designs were the first innovations in classical strings instruments for 200 years.

Strings, sampling, and synthesis

It is possible to use many string instruments to "trigger" electronically created (synthesized) or stored (sampled) sounds by using a special **pickup** system. This converts the sound of the instrument into computer data using a computer language called **MIDI** (Musical Instrument Digital Interface). Performance artist Laurie Anderson has used a violin in this way.

Glossary

acoustic referring to sound; an unamplified instrument

amplify to make louder

avant-garde modern and experimental

Baroque cultural period in Europe in the seventeenth and eighteenth centuries

bass lowest range of notes in general use; stringed instrument with the lowest range

bouzouki Greek fretted string instrument

bow stick with a length of rosined hair attached that is used for playing certain stringed instruments

bridge sharp vertical edge on a stringed instrument over which the strings are stretched

Cajun type of folk music played in Louisiana

chamber music classical music arranged for small groups of instrumentalists

clavichord instrument that has strings struck by metal hammers operated by a keyboard

concerto piece of music written for an orchestra and usually featuring a single instrumental soloist

contrabass pitch range lower than bass

damper device that muffles the sound of strings

drone string string that produces a single continuous note

electronic pickup device like a microphone that "collects" the sound from an electric stringed instrument

ensemble small group of musicians

fingerboard surface of the neck of a stringed instrument, upon which the strings are held down to change the notes

fret small strip of metal, wood, or gut on the fingerboard of a stringed instrument, across which the strings are held when changing the notes

Gaelic referring to Irish (or occasionally Scottish) culture or language

gear toothed wheel that transmits movement

gourd rounded plant that can be dried and hollowed out inside

harmonic extra note that can be heard when a main note is played

headstock part of a guitar on which the tuning pegs (or "machine heads") are usually fixed

lute round-backed instrument that preceded the guitar

lyre square, harplike instrument

mandolin small, steel-strung, fretted instrument

MIDI stands for Musical Instrument Digital Interface; a type of computer language that allows some electronic instruments to exchange data with computers and with each other

mute to muffle or quiet a sound

neck thin part of a stringed instrument along which the strings are stretched

octave eight tones that make up a musical scale

pegbox part of a stringed instrument onto which the tuning pegs are attached

pick small, flat object used to pluck the strings of certain stringed instruments

pickup *see* electronic pickup

pitch highness or lowness of a note

pizzicato action of plucking the strings of an orchestral stringed instrument that is normally bowed

psaltery early zither

qanun Turkish zither

repertoire music written for particular instruments, voices, or groups

resonator hollow object or structure used to amplify the sound of an instrument

rosin sticky substance applied to the hair on a bow, allowing it to produce friction when drawn across an instrument's strings

solo section or piece of music featuring a single performer with a group; one person performing alone is called a soloist

sonata composition for a single instrument, generally with a keyboard accompaniment (although keyboard sonatas are solo works)

soundbox hollow object or structure used to amplify the sound of an instrument

stop to change the pitch of a string by holding it down at a point along its length

string quartet classical ensemble that usually consists of two violins, a viola, and a cello

sympathetic string string that is not played directly but that makes a sound by picking up vibrations from other strings

symphony orchestra largest type of classical orchestra

tailpiece part on the body of some stringed instruments onto which the strings are fixed

tension tightness

tone quality of a sound

treble having high pitch

vellum type of very thin leather

virtuoso musician of exceptional ability

West/ern North America and the countries of Europe; of or relating to North America and the countries of Europe

Further Reading

Barber, Nicola (ed.). *The Kingfisher Young People's Book of Music.* New York: Larousse Kingfisher Chambers, 1999.

Dearling, Robert. *String Instruments: Encyclopedia of Musical Instruments.* Broomall, Penn.: Chelsea House Publishers, 2000.

Rowe, Julian. *Music.* Chicago: Heinemann Library, 1998.

Index